Runes

*A Beginner's Guide to Divination
and Reading Runes*

Table of Contents

Introduction

Runes have a rich history of mysticism that is interwoven and cannot be separated from their origins in Norse mythology. Even the gods did not comprehend the meaning of the symbols when they first encountered their use, going to great lengths to learn the mysteries these shapes held.

These symbols hold more meaning than simply a shape representing a sound in writing and can have strong magic when used for spell casting and divination. In the following chapters we will explore the deeper meanings of runes. You will soon discover how they are connected to Norse deities, and what their greater associations to nature are.

You'll also learn how to make a set of casting runes and find out different ways of using them for creating amulets, protection spells, and divination. Whether you are using runes in ceremonial rituals as part of a Norse pagan religious practice, are a student of history that wants to learn about the cultural impact of Germanic tribes or are simply focusing on the magical and divinatory aspects, this guide will explain all you need to know. Let's dive in!

Chapter One: What Are Runes?

Runes are a pre-Christianity Germanic tribal alphabet and Norse pagan symbology. Runes were used for both written communication (though limited in this scope), and spell casting.

The term "rune" holds multiple meanings:

Rune identifies the specific type of written alphabet the shapes create. Just as Cyrillic and Latin identify the types of letterforms contained in their respective alphabets.

Rune means a symbol with a mysterious or magical connotation.

Rune refers to small pieces inscribed or marked with said symbols.

The word itself evolved from the Old Norse *run*. The variation, rune, used in Modern English hasn't changed much from the Old English form. Old German, Danish, Celtic, and even Welsh forms of the word have all been closely the same to *run* or *rune*. And all have held similar meanings of secret, mysterious, magical signs.

The multi-faceted aspect of the term simply reflects the multi-leveled meaning of each symbol. At one level the symbols are simply shapes used to convey a piece of language– a visual representation of sound. On another level, each symbol has a relationship to a specific god within the Norse pantheon and associations with nature. On yet another level again, each symbol holds a deeper magical intention.

Influencing fate

Runes have always been linked to fate and seen as a way to redirect, or influence destiny.

In Norse mythology, the World Tree, Yggdrasil, was cared for by three maiden giantesses called the Norns. They were Urd, Verdandi, and Skuld, names that mean *"fate,"* *"to become,"* and *"future."* The Norns lived by the banks of the Well of Wyrd, or fate, and are similar to the fates from other mythologies in that there were three of them, they are frequently depicted as each a different age: youth, adult, and old; and they wove threads that influenced a person's future.

They were greatly respected and connected with pregnancy and birth. Norns were present at every birth, where they would determine the child's destiny and measure its thread of life. As a ritual to honor the Norns, for the first meal after giving birth, women would have a special porridge prepared for them.

Every morning the Norns collected damp earth and clay from the edges of the well and coated the roots and bark of Yggdrasil to heal the tree from any damage and to prevent the tree from beginning to rot. They would also carve symbols into the clay and the bark of the tree as sigils of protection and health, and to direct the fate of the tree and all beings who lived in the Nine Realms. These symbols were the runes.

Runes were a carved language with messages being inscribed into surfaces as opposed to being written with ink on parchment. The sharp angular shapes of the forms reflect this carved nature with lines reminiscent of a chisel bit. Runes were carved into wood, stone, metal, and bone. If there were Old Norse forms of written runes (ink on parchment or another surface) they did not survive or are yet to be discovered. The earliest historic examples of written runes on parchment date to the ninth century, and not again until the thirteenth century when there was an interest in documenting Viking Age poetry.

Our knowledge of what individual runes mean comes from Rune Poems that were written down during the medieval ages. The *Poetic Edda*, an expansive source of Norse and Viking mythology from Iceland, was also documented during this time. It's important to note these poems most likely originated from a long oral tradition, and their actual age and time of origin is unknown. The exact purpose of these poems is also unknown, but they were most likely mnemonic devices for learning the Futharks.

The Germanic worldview included that speaking a thought made that thought a part of reality. One could influence the outcome of events by speaking intentions and desired outcomes. Essentially, words created reality.

Writing fixes a thought or (the concept of) a sound in a location so that others can witness it while not being in the same place, or at the same time as the person who is speaking. If words create reality, and writing fixes that reality in place, writing is inherently magical. Thus, by their nature, runes are intrinsically magical.

Futharks

Runes belong in sets called Futharks. Just as the term alphabet is derived from the first two letters of the Greek alphabet– *alpha* and *beta*– the term Futhark is created from the first six runic letters– *feoh, ur, thorn, ansur, rad,* and *ken.*

The Elder Futhark was used with little form variations for approximately 300 years. There are twenty-four rune shapes in the Elder Futhark. (*These will be explored in detail later on.*) The Anglo-Saxon Futhark appeared in the British Isles and is likely to have come through Frisia. The Anglo-Saxon Futhark added shapes. Along with the original twenty-four runes, nine additional runes were added over time for a Futhark of thirty-three symbols.

The Younger Futhark, which developed in Scandinavian countries, was popular during the Viking Age (800-1200 BCE) and has fewer rune shapes. With only sixteen symbols, but more variations per symbol, many of the individual runes represent more than one sound. The Viking Age brought with it widespread trade and increased literacy. The Younger Futhark used during this time through Sweden, Norway, Denmark, and Iceland, became known as the alphabet of the Norsemen.

Translating runic carvings can prove tricky in that there didn't seem to be any established rules of composition. Runes could be written from left to right, or from right to left - sometimes even in the same engraving! Runes also have appeared written in mirror image form, but never upside down. Runes have no upper- and lower-case forms to help distinguish the beginnings of words or phrases, and there were no conventions regarding spaces between words or phrases. At times, runes would also be combined to form ligatures. Some carvers would include a dot or even a series of stacked dots between words, but this practice was not consistent across the regions that used runes.

Chapter Two: The History of Runes

Odin discovers the meanings of runes

Odin the Allfather, is credited for uncovering the secrets of the runes and bringing that knowledge to mankind. In Norse mythology, runes had always existed but were not understood by the gods. Their meanings were mysterious and known to hold magical powers.

The *Rúnatal*, a passage from the Old Norse poem *Hávamál* (thirteenth century CE, most likely originating from an oral tradition dating back before the Viking Age), is the story of how Odin learned the secrets of the runes.

The Norse pantheon holds two tribes of gods, the Aesir and the Vanir. Odin was ruler of the Aesir gods and considered to be one of the leading gods of the Norse pantheon. He was a god of war, poetry, and death. He favored those who displayed intelligence, creativity, and competence, and was the patron deity to both outlaws and rulers. He held no interest in justice or convention, preferring magic and cunning. As a god of war, he was not interested in the glorious purpose of a battle, but in the chaos of the fight. Berserkers— warriors who would enter into a crazed state of animal-like madness and rage during battle— were considered Odin's men.

Odin was known to take long absences from Asgard on quests of self-interests. He was obsessed with acquiring knowledge, wisdom, and magical power.

The gods of Asgard would join for council meetings around the Well of Wyrd at the base of Yggdrasil. Mimir - not a god himself, possibly a giant, or a being of time - was a counselor to the gods and lived at the Well of Wyrd. The water in the well was said to contain cosmic knowledge that would be imparted to anyone who drank from it. Odin gouged out and sacrificed his own eye in exchange for the opportunity to drink from Mimir's well, demonstrating just how obsessed he was with acquiring knowledge.

As a deity, Odin is full of contradictions. He is followed by those seeking dignity and nobility, yet he was selfish and duplicitous. It is fitting that he is called the Allfather; not only was he the father of all the gods, but he was considered to be the divine force of life itself.

At the center of the Norse universe is the World Tree, Yggdrasil. The *Poetic Edda* identifies Yggdrasil as a mighty ash tree, taller than the clouds, snow-capped like the mountains, and with fierce winds whipping around its high branches. The Nine Realms of gods, men, and other beings are amongst its branches and roots. Asgard, the home of the Aesir gods, was high in the branches. The roots of Yggdrasil ran through Midgard, the realm of mankind, Jotunheim, the realm of giants, and deep into the underworld.

Its roots and branches were home to magical beasts and beings. Nidhogg, a dragon, lived among the roots with several snakes. Ratatosk, a squirrel, ran up and down the trunk, and in and about the branches. Four stags, Dainn, Dvalinn, Duneyrr, and Durathror, lived among the branches. And an eagle flew over the tree and roosted in the highest of branches. Even a goat, called Heidrun, lived among them. All these creatures fed upon the leaves and bark of Yggdrasil.

The Norns, three maidens who lived among the roots and around the Well of Wyrd, tended to Yggdrasil. They would coat the bark with clay and inscribe symbols to protect and keep the tree healthy and strong, preserving the tree at the center of their universe. These marks also shaped the fates of those who lived in the Nine Realms.

When Odin saw the marks the Norns made on Yggdrasil, he wanted to know their meanings. The marks the Norns made were the runes. The meaning of the runes would only be revealed to those proven worthy. Odin decided that he needed to know the mysterious meanings of these symbols and was even willing to die for this information. He had already proven he was willing to sacrifice much in his pursuit of wisdom, having previously given an eye.

He sacrificed himself to the tree by hanging himself from the branches and running himself through with his spear. He forbade any help from other gods and took no water. For nine days, he hung and stared into the depths of the well. Toward the end of his ordeal, and on the verge of true death, the forms and deeper meanings of the runes were revealed to him.

It is said that with the knowledge of the runes Odin was able to use their magic to create poetry, to heal the wounded and ill, to make the weapons of enemies useless, to seduce a lover, to protect, and many other mighty deeds.

Historic origins

Many theories exist today as to the origins of the development and appearance of the runic written form. Some place the origins of runes far back into ancient times and imply a connection to ancient civilizations. The most widely accepted theories revolve around a blending of early Germanic symbols with Old Italic forms from Mediterranean civilizations.

Runes have always held a deep association with the Norse god Odin. This connection could possibly stem from the connection of Odin being the patron deity for Germanic tribal warriors. These military fighting groups would have been the ones to have encountered groups from southern Mediterranean countries. As such, these tribal warriors would have been the first Northern Europeans to encounter Greek and Old Italic writing styles.

Written scripts from antiquity could have easily influenced the development of runes, especially because they had similar shapes. These include Phoenician, Western Greek, Etruscan, and other Italic languages, including Old Latin.

The potential first evidence of Runes dates back to 50 CE with an inscription on a brooch, however, the inscription is not clear and could also be Roman. Confirmed runic inscriptions don't appear for yet another hundred years in the mid-second century. The earliest datable appearance of a runic inscription appears on the Vimose comb from Denmark. The earliest known appearance of the full Elder Futhark in order, dates approximately to 400 CE on the Kylver runestone in Sweden. There are less than 400 known surviving examples of the Elder Futhark in use.

Were there earlier examples of runes? Possibly. If runes were carved into organic materials such as wood or bone, the deterioration of those materials leaves historians without dateable samples.

Timeline

The following provides a rough timeline of the appearance and use of runes. All dates are approximate and Common Era-CE.

Early Germanic Iron Age *(prior to 350)*
50- Meldorf Brooch, possible first appearance of runes- could be Latin
160- 800 Elder Futhark
160- Vimose Comb
400- Kylver Stone- runestone with entire Elder Futhark carved in order

Migration Period *(circa 350 to circa 550)*
400-1000 Anglo-Saxon Futhark use in the British Isles
Vendel Era/Merovingian Age *(circa 550 to circa 800)*
mid to late 700s Christian Missionaries arrive in Scandinavia
Viking Age *(circa 800 to 1066)*
800- Younger Futhark use in Scandinavia
mid 800s *Abecedarium Nordmannicum* lists names of runes (unclear if this is a Rune Poem)
900- *Codex Vindobonensis 795* includes Anglo-Saxon Rune Poem
976- Harald Bluetooth raises the Jelling Stone, and runestones become fashionable
1017- runes banned in England

1066- End of Viking Age with Olof Skötkonung, the last Scandinavian king, to convert to Christianity

Medieval/ Middle Ages and later

1200s- Norwegian Rune Poem

1270- *Codex Regius* Manuscript of the *Poetic Edda,* including *Hávamál*

1400s- Icelandic Rune Poems

1600s- the Church bans the use of runes

Chapter Three: The Use of Runes

The uses of runes range widely, from telling tales of daring deeds and identifying property to instilling magical powers in weapons and creating protective talismans. Their use as a written language encompassed both the mundane and the magical.

Early uses of runes were simply names on objects, either to identify the owner or the maker of the item. Runes used for sending messages were carved on long sticks, called staves. While staves were identified in stories to be used for rune casting, and surviving relics support this, others seemed to be used for learning, with the Younger Futhark listed in order, while some carried messages such as I.O.U.s, prayers, and (somewhat salacious) love notes.

Runes have appeared on coins and personal objects such as combs and jewelry, including brooches, rings, and belts. They have been used on boxes and weapons. Runes have been found carved on wood, whalebone, antlers, and in stone.

Runestones

The largest, and possibly most well-known examples of the use of runes are runestones. These are free-standing, multi-ton rocks carved with runes and decorations. The tradition of memorial stones is named in the poem, the *Hávamál*, which tells the story of how Odin learned the meanings of runes.

Runestones appeared as early as the fourth century but did not gain popularity until the mid-tenth century when the Danish King Harald Bluetooth raised the Jelling Stone in commemoration of his parents. The majority of runestones were carved between the mid 900s and the end of the Viking Age.

There are over three thousand runestones, with the vast majority of them located in Sweden. There are 250 located in Denmark, fifty in Norway, and none in Iceland. However, runestones appeared as far afield as the Germanic tribes traveled and have been identified near the Black Sea to the east, and on the Isle of Man to the west.

These commemorative stones were intended to be seen. They would have carvings on multiple sides and frequently included decorative elements of beasts and people. The carvings would be painted with bright colors, and they would be placed in locations such as along waterways, at intersections, and at bridges, where they would be accessible to people.

Runestones were raised to memorialize the great achievements of people. Stones would be erected by rich families, usually by surviving spouses and children to honor husbands, fathers, wives, or notable members of their tribes. Frequently they would be for the dead, but they were not tombstones. Runestones were not limited to the dead, and the living would also raise a stone to boast of their deeds.

The inscriptions followed a set pattern. First, who commissioned the stone was named. Then, who the stone was honoring, and their deeds and accomplishments— why they were being memorialized. Frequently this section would be composed in verse. Sometimes a prayer would be included, or a mystical passage for bearing the dead to the next world, or both. Lastly, the name of the runemaster would be included. As Christianity grew in influence through the Viking Age, runestones would include Christian prayers as well.

While the practice of runestones ended with the Viking Age, runic inscriptions on smaller objects continued. Christian practices during the Viking Age, and after, did not discourage the inclusion of runes alongside Latin writings on such symbolic items as crosses and coffins. It is speculated this was done from one of two perspectives. The first being as an attempt to ease Norse pagans into welcoming Christianity. The second, as an attempt by Norse pagans to indicate they were familiar with Christian tenets and included them with the hope that the church would leave them alone. Combining runes with Latin inscriptions continued until the church banned the practice in the seventeenth century.

Magical practices

There are several magical practices that make use of runes. Divination, or the reading of runes was one way a person could question and discover the intentions of their fate. Staves, bones, or small stones inscribed with the Futhark were used for this type of reading.

Runes were also used for spells. They would be used for enchantments of health and protection among other purposes. Spellcasting inscriptions combined the runes for specific outcomes and intentions. Those inscriptions would be carved on a talisman or on other items. Warriors would have inscriptions made on their weapons for strength and prowess on the battlefield, or so that the weapon would bring a swift death to their enemies. They would name their swords and spears and have those names inscribed into the weapon, embedding the item with power.

Spellcasting, amulets, and divinatory uses of runes will be explored later in this book.
While runes were used for magical intent as part of spellcasting or divining the future, they were also seen as being magical in and of themselves.

A word of caution

Magical practices with runes should never be fooled around with. Even the Old Norse poems warn against working with runes if not fully versed in their meanings: *Let no man carve runes to cast a spell, save first he learns to read them well.*

During the Viking Age, both men and women of richer families knew how to read and write runes. However, when they needed the work of rune casting – runes specifically for magical intent – they would hire a runemaster. Runemasters not only carved more complex examples of rune work, such as runestones, but they were also well educated in the deeper meanings of runes to be able to properly implement their magical properties.

Remember, runes are linked to Odin, and he made their meanings available to humans. He is a god of the chaotic aspects of war, is tricky, and is linked to things dark and dangerous. Runes cast incorrectly, even with the best of intentions, can be dangerous and bring harm to the unprepared.

A passage from the *Poetic Edda* tells of a runemaster, who in his travels encounters a man with a gravely ill daughter. The runemaster discovers that she has a rune carved talisman of whalebone that has been poorly executed. The person who made the talisman may have intended it to be for good luck or good health, but they did not fully understand what they were doing. This resulted in the talisman causing the young woman to be sick. The young woman instantly recovered as soon as the runemaster destroyed the malicious runes and provided a properly created rune cast.

This cautionary tale should not be taken lightly. This guide only provides an introduction to the use of runes. Runes are a part of an active reclamation of cultural heritage. Approach them with the care you would take when learning about any culture outside of your own. It is recommended before fully engaging in rune casting to continue and expand your study of the cultural and religious background of Norse and Germanic pagan practices.

Use with respect

Symbols from the Elder Futhark have been taken and used by political groups in the twentieth and twenty-first centuries. Those groups want to align with the intrinsic power of the symbol and be seen as having that same energy. When runic shapes are used as a symbol that has nothing to do with their original intent, the meaning can be tainted. This incorrect and often negative/harmful association can put those who use the symbols in their religious practices at risk.

Chapter Four: Making Your Own Runes

Rune sets can be purchased from many sources. New Age stores and practitioners online provide many options for hand-crafted sets. They are even available from mass-produced sources. However, the strongest runes that will read true for you are ones that you have made yourself. Runes are a very personal item, and much like tarot cards, you don't want someone else touching or "playing" with them.

If you choose to purchase a set, you will want to cleanse them and personalize them before use. The cleansing of runes will be discussed later in this chapter.

Definitions: In this chapter, we will explore creating rune sets. (Rune stones, not to be confused with runestones, the massive free-standing rocks, typically refer to sets carved in stone, engraved, or painted onto ceramic or glass. The name rune staves is typically used for sets carved in wood. For simplicity, both are referred to as 'sets' or simply as 'runes' in this chapter, following the definition that refers to small pieces inscribed or marked with said symbols.

When creating your own rune set for casting and divination, it is important that you first familiarize yourself with the shapes of the runes and practice creating them. Start by practicing with paper and pencil. Trace out the forms for each shape. You want the lines to be straight and equally spaced. You can start by practicing on gridded paper. The lines will help to keep your forms straight and even.

You may have seen examples of runes with curved lines, such as a Feoh with two branches curving up to the right instead of as straight lines angling up to the right. Runes with curved lines are from the Anglo-Saxon or Younger Futharks and evolved into having stylized curved branches because they were eventually written. For casting runes, you want to stay as close to the original forms used by the Norns, and so sticking with the straight-lined style of the Elder Futhark is important.

If grid paper is not available, you may find a ruler helpful to use as a straight-edge guide and to ensure your line lengths are even. You can also mark out your own length guides along the edge of a second sheet of paper, instead of using a ruler.

After you are done practicing for that session, erase or mark through all of your practice shapes, and burn the paper. Do not doodle runes onto the edges of papers or on forms you need to keep, or on anything you will be handing to other people.

Remember, the runes themselves are inherently magical, and an incorrectly created rune could cause harm.

When you are more confident regarding the rune shapes, you will want to practice again using the materials you intend on creating your set with. Carving tools, wood-burning and even drawing in clay all take different muscle control than paper and pencil, so practice is crucial. These first practice runes should be destroyed, and not left. Depending on the materials you have chosen to create your runes with, you will either need to scrape/erase and burn your practice work, or wipe off and sanitize the surface.

Materials

Runes work best when made from natural materials: wood, clay, or stones. Other materials can also be used but proceed with caution. Metals hold onto negative energy that can be difficult to cleanse. Synthetic materials do not hold the magic as well, and the inherent manufactured nature of the material could taint the runes.

A caution regarding stones: this includes semi-precious stones and crystals. Materials from the earth can hold onto strong earth magic. Crystals have their own magical energies, so you want to ensure their properties align with the rune you intend to use on them. Also, some crystals and semi-precious stones are mined from the earth. If you choose to use these, make sure you are using ethically sourced materials.

River stones are a good choice of stone because they have been cleansed in natural running water. Glass is also considered an earth stone since it is made from sand. Since it is clear and is without an internal structure like crystals, it easily accepts the magical charges given to it.

The best materials to choose are the ones that reflect the original nature of runes: wood and clay. The Norns carved runes on the World Tree, the mighty ash — also sometimes thought to be a yew tree. And they coated the trunk and roots of the World Tree with clay.

Any wood can be used. Ash and yew are the top choices as those reflect the World Tree, and elm (the first man and woman were carved from ash and elm) would be the woods that resonate with the highest rune energy. Branches you cut yourself are going to be a better choice than wood that has been pre-milled from another source.

Clay rune stones also will hold high rune magic. However, working with clay poses an issue in that not everyone has access to a kiln for the high temperature firing process.

The *Hávamál* describes the process of cutting, carving, scratching, and staining runes. Runestones, rune stones, and rune staves traditionally have paint in the grooves for increased visibility. Red is the leading popular color of runes, however during the Viking Age they had access to many different pigments, and runes were painted many different colors. The nature of *cutting, carving,* and *scratching* implies wood or stone. This is not to say you cannot paint runes onto small glass pebbles, which can be very pretty indeed. Be mindful of the levels of magical energy you will be tapping into with different materials.

Making rune stones

Once you have become familiar with the materials you have chosen to work with and are confident that you will be able to craft your runes properly, you can begin. The act of creation itself is a magic ritual, and you should be aware of all intentions as you work.

Before you begin, make sure you have a proper work area. Clear away unnecessary clutter and have all of your desired tools within reach. You will want a workspace free of distractions, where you can focus. Be sure you will have an adequate amount of time for this process. If you don't have a large block of time to create all twenty-four symbols of the Elder Futhark at once, divide your work into processes (such as measuring and cutting wood), and then into working the three Aetts, focusing on only creating eight runes at a time. This may mean you have to work at times when others in your household are away, or asleep.

The runes the Norns carved into Yggdrasil were to protect, heal, and maintain the health of the World Tree. Be mindful of thoughts of this nature and think of your intent when creating your runes. You may like to practice a centering ritual before you begin work. This may include saying a prayer to the Aesir gods, Odin the Allfather, or a simple mind-clearing meditation. You may choose to burn a white candle and play calming music, or recordings of forest or other nature sounds. Your mental state and intentions should be calm and focused. If you are agitated, have dark, angry thoughts, or are overly sad and upset, you could feed these negative energies into your runes, and all castings or readings made with that set could potentially have negative or harmful outcomes, even after cleansing your runes.

Knowledge of the runes was gained from an act of sacrifice. Be giving of something while making your rune stones. Pour out a drink and offer it up as tribute— do not drink it, but instead, sacrifice it to the ground— the Aesir gods liked beer. At the very least the runes deserve all of your intention and focus. If you accidentally injure yourself and bleed during the process, stop. You will need to destroy the runes you bled on. Blood magic is powerful and dangerous, especially to the untrained. As a beginner of any magical practice, you do not want to accidentally engage in blood magic.

Making your own runes can be fun and satisfying. Instructions for two different types of rune sets are provided below for varying skill levels.

Glass runes (beginner techniques)

Materials: clear glass pebbles, colored and clear fingernail polish, or paint and clear gloss acrylic sealer, rubbing alcohol

Tools: thin paint brushes

Sourcing materials: Glass pebbles can be purchased from arts and craft stores, home décor shops, or most shops with floral departments, and can be ordered online. Fingernail polish can be purchased from most drug and beauty supply shops. Paint, markers, and sealants can be purchased from art and craft supply shops. Do not get frosted glass pebbles, as the process described here will cover that over with a gloss coating, ruining the matte effect.

Clear glass pebbles are recommended because the use of colored glass pebbles brings in the aspects of color magic to your runes. Research color associations to the runes and color magic before selecting colored pebbles.

You will want to work in an area with good ventilation, and where clean-up will be easy. Tarps and surface covers are recommended. Paint and fingernail polish damage furniture, so plan your workspace accordingly. If you use a spray sealer, you will want to spray outside, and use a face covering.

- Cleanse your glass pebbles *(see end of chapter)*.
- Clean your glass pebbles with rubbing alcohol to remove any oils.

For runes on top of glass pebbles:

- Draw your runes on paper to the size of the glass pebble. For runes on top of the pebble, draw the runes right-reading.

- Place the glass pebble over the drawing of the rune on paper, and using a thin paintbrush, trace the shape onto the glass with the nail polish or paint. Most glass pebbles have a slightly domed side and a flat side. The domed side is up.

- Use a thin paintbrush for either nail polish or paint. The brushes in nail polish are too clumsy and chunky for clean line work.

For runes that are visible through the glass pebble:

- Draw your runes on paper to the size of the glass pebbles, but draw them backward/mirror image. This is so that they will read the right way round when looking through the glass.

- Place your glass pebble upside down (dome side down) over the drawing, and using a thin paintbrush trace the shape onto the bottom of the glass pebble with polish or paint.

- Allow drying between coats. It may take several coats of polish/paint to get an intensely colored line.

- Apply clear coating; paint a few coatings of clear polish over your rune marking. (The brush that comes in the polish is good for this since this isn't detailed work). Or alternatively you can use a clear coat acrylic sealer. If using the spray-on kind, spray outdoors.

- Dispose of your pre-drawn runes appropriately.

Wooden runes (advanced techniques)

Materials: A 1- to 2-inch-thick branch, minimum 13 inches in length (for 24 x 1cm or .5-inch disks— you will want extra in case of miscuts) or 24 wood disks* (plus extras for practice), wood-stain or paint.

Tools: sandpaper in increasingly higher grit count, hand saw, carving tools: V-tool/U-gouge or wood-burning tool, clamps, ruler, pencil, thin paintbrush, safety glasses.

You will want to work in an area with good ventilation and where clean-up will be easy. You may find working outside during woodcutting is best. Tarps and surface covers are recommended. Wood carving, wood burning, and staining can damage furniture, so plan your workspace accordingly. *If you use purchased wood disks you will want to cleanse them before working with them.*

Sourcing wood: You can use branches you find on your outings or check for yard clean-up piles from trimmed trees. (It's always best to be polite and ask before you take a branch from someone's property.)

Do not cut living branches from trees, as this could be dangerous if you don't know exactly what you are doing. You could be injured, and it could cause harm to the tree. (Harming trees is counter to the original intention of runes, as the Norns used them to heal and protect Yggdrasil.)

Know the laws regarding taking branches from parks in your area. It is illegal to take branches (even ones that fell naturally) from the National Parks in the United States and Canada due to natural ecological conservancy policies.

You can order branches with bark still on them from craft stores or ask at your local lumber yard. Do not cut green wood. Let your branches fully dry before creating your runes. Depending on local temperature and climate this can take several days to several weeks.

- Wear safety glasses when using woodworking tools.
- Protect your work surfaces as needed.

Creating wood disks:

- Find a section of branch that has an even thickness. You may need several branches to have enough wood for twenty-four runes. Using a ruler, measure out the desired thickness for your runes. Thinner sections will be more difficult to cut.

- Brace the branch against a worktable or a sawhorse. Have the section you wish to cut hang over the empty space. Using a back-and-forth motion, saw off 24 disks, plus enough for several pieces to practice on.

- Remember the old adage "measure twice, cut once."

- If you purchased pre-cut disks, cleanse them before working the runes into their surface.

Preparing the surface:

- Use sandpaper to smooth the surfaces of wood disks (this applies to both hand-cut and store purchased). Start with coarse sandpaper, and gradually work through increasingly higher grit counts to smooth the wood to a silky, burr-free polish.

- Plan your runes.

- Using a pencil, carefully draw the rune form onto one side of the wood disk (the other side will stay blank).

Wood burning:

- Following instructions from the wood-burning tool, carefully trace over your pencil drawing.

- If you have never used wood-burning tools before, be sure to practice on scrap wood.

Wood carving:

- Carving tools are very sharp. Never carve toward your torso or hand.

- If you have never used carving tools before, be sure to practice on scrap wood.

- Clamp the prepared wood disk to a stable work surface.

- Place the tip of the carving tool against the wood. Apply pressure down into the wood and away from your body following the pencil-drawn shape.

- V-shaped and U-shaped carving tools will cut into the wood creating the shape of their name, providing either a sharp indent or a smooth curved inscribed line.

- Do not dig the carving tip into the wood. Do not press the top of the V or U shape below the surface of the wood disk, as this can cause chips, and get the carving tool stuck.

- Do carve lightly and go over the lines multiple times to achieve a deeper groove in the wood.

- After burning or carving, sand the surface again to remove any burrs.

- Stain or paint.

- Using a thin paintbrush, carefully trace the etched lines of your runes.

- Allow drying in a dust-free area for at least twenty-four hours. Test for stain/paint dryness before cleansing and charging your runes.

Cleansing your runes

You will want to cleanse any purchased rune sets or materials you plan on using to make your own rune sets before beginning. You will also want to cleanse the rune set you have made when you are finished and again before you begin using them.

Cleansing runes helps to clear out negative energies or residual magic that may have worked their way into the rune stone. You want to remove these old energies before charging your stones with your magical energies.

You may find that you want to cleanse your stones after conducting readings for some people, or if you feel they have been mistreated or handled excessively by others.
There are many ways to cleanse your runes. Exposing them to the forces of natural elements is the most basic. Depending on the material, you can let them rest in the natural running water of a stream or creek, or in the rain. Do not attempt to cleanse them in running tap water, or a stagnant pond.

You can let them sit out all night under a full moon. Or place them in the early morning sun and let them sit outside for a full day and night. If you do not have a safe outside place to rest your stones, they can sit in a windowsill where they have full access to the natural light.

Other ways of cleansing your stones involve knowledge of other magics, so in this case, keeping it simple is best. Work with the cleansing method that best fits your situation and resonates with your practice.

You will need a soft drawstring bag of natural fibers such as cotton or silk. You will want to keep them in a place that is your own, and not a location in your home where others have access and will be moving your stones to gain access to something else. You want the runes to absorb your energy and not the confusing energies of multiple people.

Charging your runes

Every step along the way of creating your runes has been a ritual, and this is no different. Be sure to have uninterrupted time and a location where you can work. Clear your mind of unnecessary worries and concerns at this time and hold space and intention for what you are doing.

There are many ways to charge your runes. Smudging is the practice of having the smoke of specific herbs wash over an item. Sage is a cleansing herb and is well suited for this. You will want to cleanse the holding container for your runes as well. Hold each rune stone in the smoke and breathe the name of the rune into the piece. You do that by placing the rune close to your mouth and speaking the name of the rune. Be sure to have your breath involved so the air from your lungs caresses the rune. Repeat for each rune.

When you are finished, carefully place the runes back into their bag, and put them in the place you have chosen for them.

Not everyone can tolerate smoke; fortunately, there are other ways to charge your stones. Wrap your stones in a clean cloth and bury them for a week. When you unearth them, breathe their name into them.

Another means of charging your runes is to set them out in the early morning sun and leave them for a full day cycle. When you collect the stones, be sure to breathe their names into them.

There is no prescribed set of rules that apply when cleansing and charging your stones. Use the methods that feel best to you.

Chapter Five: Elder Futhark

The Elder Futhark was the first runic alphabet. There are twenty-four rune shapes, and each shape has a name, a meaning, and a deeper intention. The term Futhark is created from the first six rune shapes. Unlike the Anglo-Saxon or Younger Futhark, the forms of the Elder Futhark are made with straight lines, not curved ones. This reflects the carved nature of how runes were carved/chiseled into stone, wood, and other items.

Runes are much more than an old form of writing with each shape representing a letter. They have connections to the Norse gods and associations with nature. Their meanings run deeper than the simple definition of their name, with each having a magical deeper meaning.

A note on names and meanings

Most runes have multiple variations of their name. This is a result of evolution and changes in language from original terms, and which version of the name was more commonly adopted. Rune history is based on Old Germanic and Old Norse traditions and locations. Language grew and changed in the various locales. Name modifications come from the variations in the Scandinavian, Danish, Icelandic, and Old English language uses. Even though all the runes in the Elder Futhark are still the original twenty-four shapes, the names you find here may vary in their origins. For example, runes that were modified and were more commonly used in the Anglo-Saxon Futhark may carry an Old English name.

Life in Old Germanic times was not easy. They did not have the resources for food, heat, and medicines that modern living provides. The Old Norse gods served many positions, and there wasn't a single war god or a single fertility god. The fertility gods were vitally important in that they were concerned with the cycles of life, including the cycle of planting and harvesting, but also human reproduction. Many of the runes have fertility as one of their aspects, and it is up to the reader's interpretation if fertility in that instance is referring to financial growth, an abundant harvest, babies (be they animals or people), or a new romantic relationship.

Godly associations are given when known. Not all runes have an association with a god or a mythological being. Many are simply forces of nature. Color associations vary widely and have different connections based on the interpretation of the runes. Plants and gemstones respond to the energy associated with their related runes. In many cases, they have a direct connection of meaning or a relationship with the associated god.

The three aetts

The Elder Futhark is divided into three groups of eight, each called an *aett*. These groupings identify runes to specific gods and concepts. A rune's position within the aett is significant in the use of coding runes, a means of writing a rune without using the exact symbol. Examples: Feoh is the first rune in the first aett 1:1; Isa is the third rune of the second aett 2:3.

(The purpose of this codifying is unclear. Were they created to add another level of mystery to the runes, or was it intended as a way to use the written/letter form aspect of a rune without enacting its magic energies? Sadly, we will never know.)

Freya's aett

Attributed to Freya and/or Frey, both of whom were considered gods of fertility and prosperity. Freya is associated with beauty, plant life, and was a practitioner of divination. Her twin brother, Frey, is associated with sunny skies and moderate rains, and good harvests. They were Vanir gods. This aett aligns with life cycle concepts. The eight runes of this aett are Feoh, Uruz, Thurisaz, Ansur, Raidho, Kenaz, Gebo, and Wunjo.

Feoh

- Meaning: cattle; wealth

- Runes originated in a time when owning cattle was a sign of wealth and property. It usually coincided with having some form of leadership or power within the community. This rune has come to mean financial wealth, but also social/community wealth. Other attributes include financial beginnings and fertility.

- Description: tall vertical line with two stacked branches approximately halfway down the side, angling up and to the right.

- Letter equivalent/sound: F

- God: Frey

- Tree: elder

- Herb: nettle

- Gemstone: moss agate

- Color associations: red, green, brown

- Position in Futhark: 1

- Position in aett: 1:1

Uruz/Ur

- Meaning: aurochs; strength

- Aurochs were a type of wild ox with extreme horns (they went extinct in the 1600s), described as being as large as an elephant (according to Julius Caesar) and as fierce as a raging bull. This rune indicates very masculine vital life energy, it indicates primal power, physical health, and sexual prowess.

- Description: vertical line with a short branch angling slightly down and to the right. From the end of the first branch a second vertical short branch goes straight down; resembles a Latin lower-case N (n).

- Letter equivalent/sound: U

- Tree: birch

- Herb: sphagnum moss

- Gemstone: carbuncle

- Color associations: dark green, red, orange

- Position in Futhark: 2

- Position in aett: 1:2

Thurisaz/Thorn

- Meaning: giant; danger, suffering

- The shape of this rune reflects one of its meanings as a thorn, a sharp deterrent. It can be meant as a warning, or as the need for defense. It can also be interpreted as a fertility rune since thorny vines will break rocks to take root. It is also a play on words for thorn: prick: phallus.

- Description: tall vertical line with two short branches aligned to the mid area of the vertical forming a peak to the right; resembles a Latin P with an extra line growing up from the top.

- Letter equivalent/sound: TH

- God: Thor

- Tree: hawthorn

- Herb: houseleek

- Gemstone: sapphire

- Color associations: red, brown, white

- Position in Futhark: 3

- Position in aett: 1:3

Ansur

- Meaning: mouth of God; prosperity and vitality

- This is the rune of communication. Odin is credited with having breathed life into the carved figures that became the first man and woman. This rune is that life-breath. It represents intelligence, divine inspiration, and insight.

- Description: tall vertical line with two stacked branches aligned to the top of the vertical, angling down and to the right; resembles a Latin F.

- Letter equivalent/sound: A

- God: Odin

- Tree: ash

- Herb: fly agaric

- Gemstone: emerald

- Color associations: dark blue, yellow

- Position in Futhark: 4

- Position in aett: 1:4

Raidho

- Meaning: ride; movement, growth

- One of the interpretations of Raidho is a wagon wheel, and it represents a journey. That journey could be a physical one from here to there, or a metaphysical journey. It also has connections to the journey from life to death. Other aspects Raidho encompasses include leadership, guidance, and moral integrity.

- Description: tall vertical line with two short branches aligned to the top of the vertical forming a peak to the right, a third short branch meets the vertical at the same point of the second branch and angles down and to the right; resembles a Latin R.

- Letter equivalent/sound: R

- God: Thor

- Tree: oak

- Herb: mugwort

- Gemstone: chrysoprase

- Color associations: red, violet, black

- Position in Futhark: 5

- Position in aett: 1:5

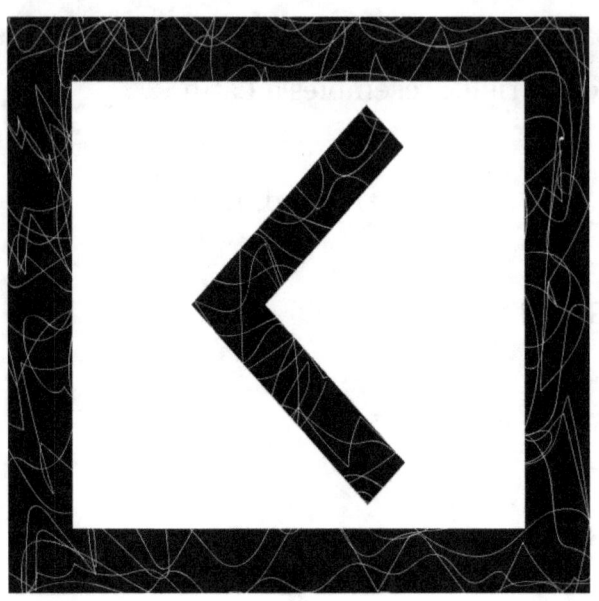

Kenaz/Ken

- Meaning: torch; illumination, knowledge

- The various names of this rune have wildly different interpretations from "fire," to "knowing," to "ulcer." One interpretation takes these seemingly disparate meanings and combines them to specifically mean medical knowledge. Kenaz represents clarity of thought, and learning through research and exploration.

- Description: junction with two short branches, one branch angles up and to the right, the other down and to the right (forming a point to the left); resembles a Latin K without the vertical.

- Letter equivalent/sound: K

- Tree: pine

- Herb: cowslip

- Gemstone: bloodstone

- Color associations: red, yellow

- Position in Futhark: 6

- Position in aett: 1:6

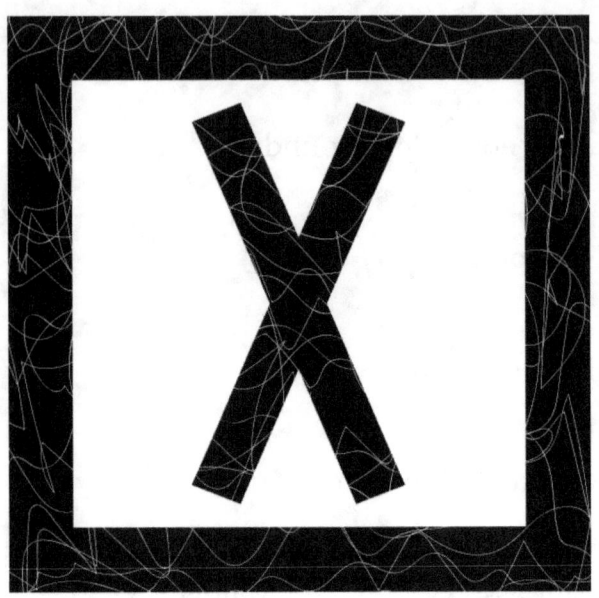

Gebo/Gyfu

- Meaning: gift; generosity

- Thought of as spiritual gifts and generosity. This rune can be interpreted as the gifts of men to gods such as sacrifice, or from gods to men: religious teachings. It encompasses concepts of fair trade, contracts, reciprocations, generosity, and harmony. It is a rune of marriage and sex.

- Description: intersection of two long branches, creating an X shape; resembles a Latin X.

- Letter equivalent/sound: G

- Tree: elm

- Herb: heartsease

- Gemstone: opal

- Color associations: dark blue, red, gold

- Position in Futhark: 7

- Position in aett: 1:7

Wunjo

- Meaning: joy; satisfaction

- This is the rune of friendship and wellbeing. It represents like-minded community and family bonding. It brings balance and harmony.

- Description: tall vertical line with two short branches aligned to the top of the vertical forming a peak to the right; resembles a Latin P.

- Letter equivalent/sound: V or W

- God: Ullr

- Tree: ash

- Herb: flax

- Gemstone: diamond

- Color associations: yellow, red

- Position in Futhark: 8

- Position in aett: 1:8

Hagal's aett

Hagal literally means hail. Based on the stanzas in the rune poems, hail is seen as destructive but also as bringing life (as it melts into water). This aett encompasses the duality of external forces of nature as they impact life. The eight runes for this aett are Hagal, Naudhiz, Isa, Gera, Eoh, Peorth, Eolh, and Sigel.

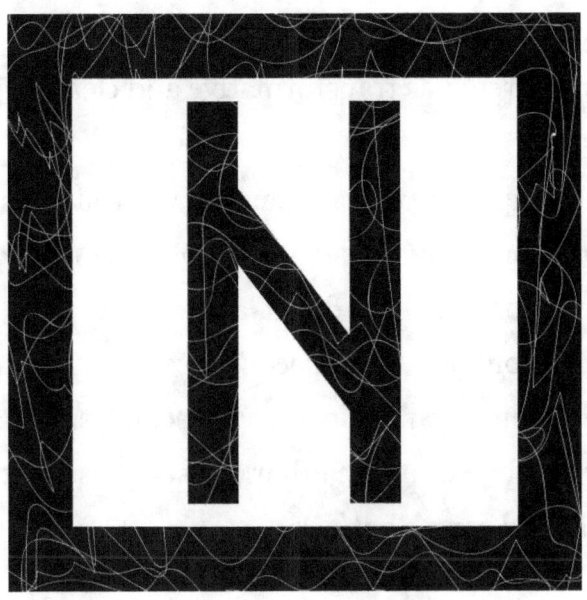

Hagal/Hagalez

- Meaning: hail; destructive natural forces

- Hagal is the destructive power of nature. It literally means hail, and what kinds of damage and rebuilding that happen in the wake of a storm. It embodies uncontrolled disruption and change. It brings a shift in energies and represents opportunity. Hagal is also the ninth rune in the Elder Futhark. Nine is a potent number in Norse mythology: There are the Nine Realms, Odin hung on Yggdrasil for nine days to learn the secret of the runes, and human gestation takes nine months. With this aspect in mind, it can be interpreted as transformative and cleansing.

- Description: two tall, parallel vertical lines with short branches aligned slightly above the midpoint on the left line, angling down and to the right, making a junction on the second vertical slightly below midpoint; variation with a second crossbar adopted from the Younger Futhark; resembles a Latin H with a slanted center bar.

- Letter equivalent/sound: H

- God: Hel

- Tree: yew

- Herb: lily of the valley

- Gemstone: onyx

- Color associations: light blue, black

- Position in Futhark: 9

- Position in aett: 2:1

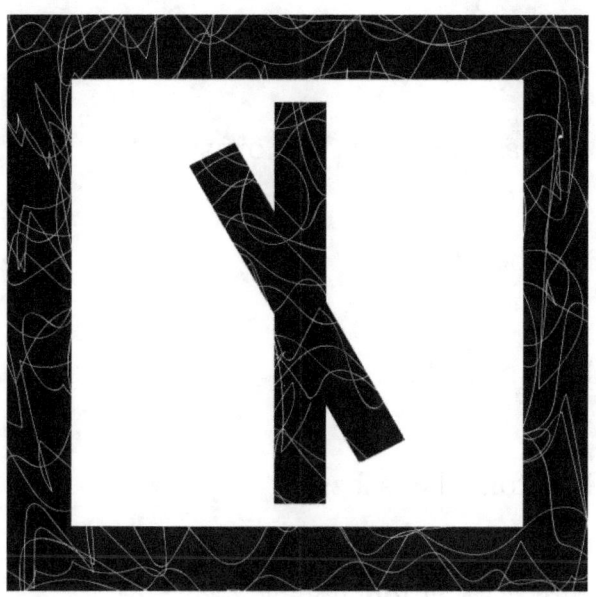

Naudhiz/Nyd

- Meaning: need; hope

- Naudiz is not the desire of want, but the need of necessity and the associated sadness and forlorn aspects of hope. This is the rune for doing what must be done, consequences, and life lessons. It has connections to longing and even lust.

- Description: a tall vertical line with a short branch intersecting at a slight downward angle on the right, forming a cross; resembles a Latin lower case Latin T (t).

- Letter equivalent/sound: N

- Being association: the Norns

- Tree: beech

- Herb: bistort

- Gemstone: lapis lazuli

- Color associations: black, gray

- Position in Futhark: 10

- Position in aett: 2:2

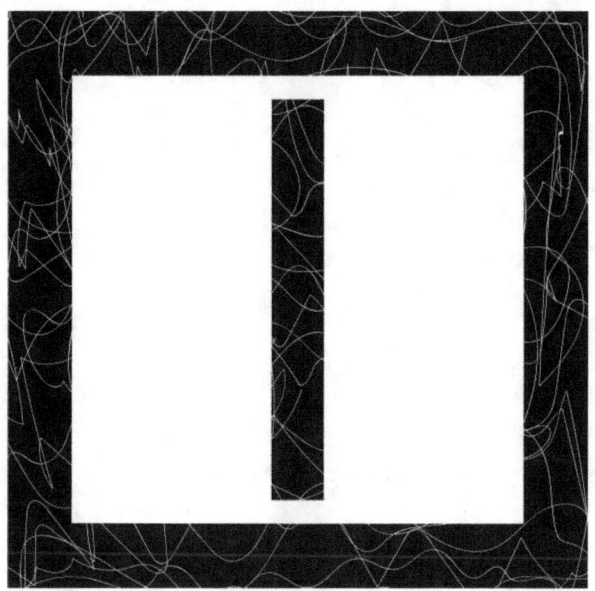

Isa

- Meaning: ice; wait, inaction

- In Scandinavia and Iceland, winter and ice are a very important part of life. One must wait out the ice. The inaction of Isa is patience, self-control.

- Description: a single tall vertical line; resembles a Latin I.

- Letter equivalent/sound: I

- Tree: alder

- Herb: henbane

- Gemstone: cats-eye

- Color associations: black, silver, brown

- Position in Futhark: 11

- Position in aett: 2:3

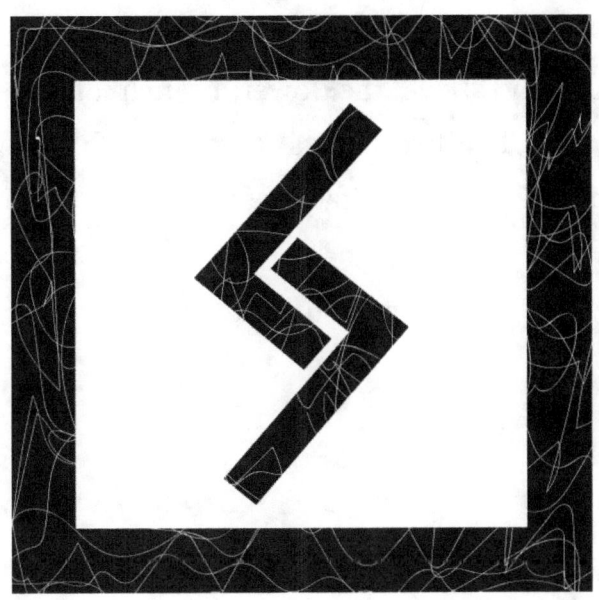

Gera/Jara

- Meaning: year; time, harvest

- This is a rune of planting, growth, and reaping rewards. Gera represents the cycle of the year. It encompasses concepts of good timing, fertility, peace, and prosperity.

- Description: a junction with two short branches, one branch angles up and to the right, the other down and to the right (forming a point to the left), a second junction of two branches in a similar configuration but in the opposite direction so the point is to the right.

The top branch of the lower, right-facing point is directly above the lower branch of the left-facing point. The two points do not touch; resembles two sideways Latin Vs facing toward each other.

- Letter equivalent/sound: Y

- Tree: oak

- Herb: rosemary

- Gemstone: carnelian

- Color associations: light blue, green

- Position in Futhark: 12

- Position in aett: 2:4

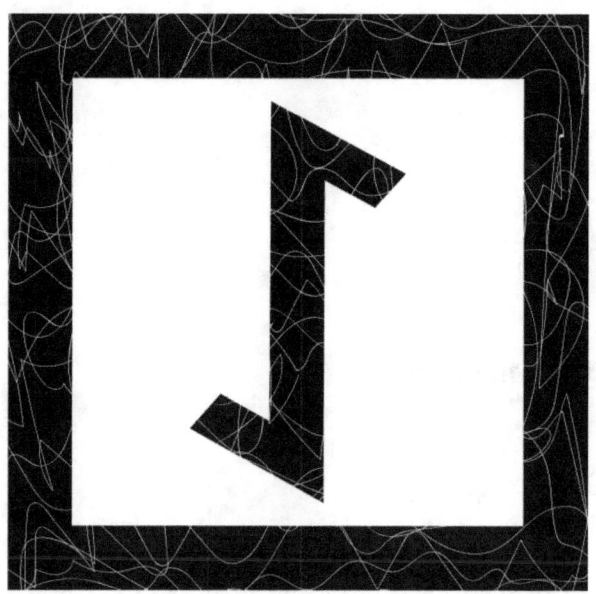

Eoh/Eihwaz

- Meaning: yew; strength

- This is a rune of wisdom and the mysteries of magic. It is a spiritual rune for communications between the magic and the mundane.

- Description: a tall vertical line with a short branch intersecting at the top of the vertical and angled down and to the right, a second short branch intersecting at the bottom of the vertical, angling up and to the left; resembles a stylized Latin S.

- Letter equivalent/sound: I

- God: Ullr

- Tree: yew

- Herb: mandrake

- Gemstone: topaz

- Color associations: dark blue, red

- Position in Futhark: 13

- Position in aett: 2:5

Peorth

- Meaning: unknown; mystery

- The actual meaning of Peorth has been lost to history. It has been associated with fruit trees, games of chance, and female sexuality and fertility. Therefore, this rune has come to embrace unexpected opportunity, the unknown, and fate. It is frequently associated with gambling and random occurrences.

- Description: a tall vertical line with a short branch intersecting at the top of the vertical and angled down and to the right, the branch then angles up and to the right; a short branch intersects at the bottom of the vertical and angles up to the right, before angling down to the right; resembles a Latin C.

- Letter equivalent/sound: P

- Being association: the Norns

- Tree: beech

- Herb: aconite

- Gemstone: aquamarine

- Color associations: black, purple

- Position in Futhark: 14

- Position in aett: 2:6

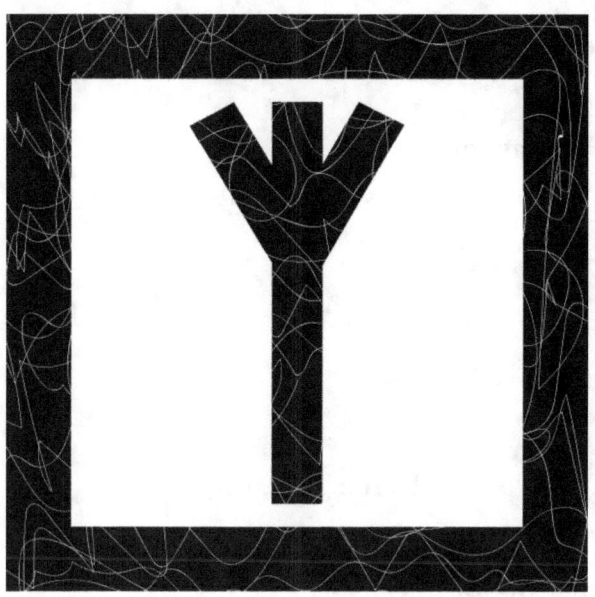

Eolh/Elhaz

- Meaning: elk; protection

- This rune is a strong protection symbol. It protects through banishment and casting-away. It has connections with perseverance in the face of adversity and higher self-consciousness.

- Description: a tall vertical line with two short branches intersecting slightly above midpoint; the left branch angles up to the left, the right branch angles up to the right; resembles a Latin Y with the vertical baseline continuing up.

- Letter equivalent/sound: Z

- Tree: aspen

- Herb: sedge

- Gemstone: amethyst

- Color associations: gold, brown

- Position in Futhark: 15

- Position in aett: 2:7

Sigel/Sowilo

- Meaning: the sun; success

- This rune represents motivation and victory. It is personal wholeness, meeting goals, and turning energy into action.

- Description: three short branches consecutively, from bottom to top: branch angles up to the right, the next branch angles up to the left, the uppermost branch angles up to the right forming a zig-zag; resembles a stylized Latin S.

- Letter equivalent/sound: S

- God: Baldur

- Tree: juniper

- Herb: mistletoe

- Gemstone: ruby

- Color associations: white, gold, yellow

- Position in Futhark: 16

- Position in aett: 2:8

Tyr's aett

Tyr was an honorable god of war, who was valiant and did not hesitate to do what was necessary for the greater good, even if at great personal cost. He distracted the wolf Fenrir, so it could be bound by the other gods, by placing his hand in the wolf's mouth. He subsequently lost the hand. This aett encompasses the concepts of internal struggles within personal control. The eight runes for this aett are Tiwaz, Beorc, Ehwaz, Mannaz, Lagu, Ing, Daeg, and Odhal.

Tiwaz

- Meaning: Tyr; victory

- Used by warriors in battle, Tyr's rune brings victory and protects from harm. This rune is associated with loyalty, righteousness, honor, and honesty. It has connections with making the right choices and developing spiritual awareness.

- Description: a tall vertical line with two short branches forming an arrow point at the top; resembles a pointy Latin T.

- Letter equivalent/sound: T

- God: Tyr

- Tree: oak

- Herb: sage

- Gemstone: coral

- Color associations: red, green

- Position in Futhark: 17

- Position in aett: 3:1

Beorc

- Meaning: birch; fertility, growth

- This is a rune of spring and rebirth. It has connections with new beginnings and growth. It also has strong maternal energy and can signify sanctuary, maturity, fertility, and childbearing.

- Description: tall vertical line with two short branches aligned to the top of the vertical forming a peak to the right, a second pair of short branches forms a second peak to the right, immediately below the first one; resembles a Latin B.

- Letter equivalent/sound: B

- God: Idun

- Tree: birch

- Herb: lady's mantle

- Gemstone: moonstone

- Color associations: dark green, blue

- Position in Futhark: 18

- Position in aett: 3:2

Ehwaz

- Meaning: horse; trust

- This rune represents the connection between a horse and rider. It represents progress through partnerships and trust, teamwork, cooperation, marriage, and sexuality.

- Description: two tall parallel vertical lines with a short branch angling down to the right from the top of the left vertical, connecting to a second short branch continuing up to the right connecting to the top of the right-most vertical line; resembles a Latin M.

- Letter equivalent/sound: E

- God: Frey or Odin

- Tree: ash

- Herb: ragwort

- Gemstone: Iceland spar

- Color associations: white, green, red

- Position in Futhark: 19

- Position in aett: 3:3

Mannaz/Man

- Meaning: mankind; cooperation

- This rune symbolizes both humankind and the individual. It represents mental preparedness and acceptance of the human condition. It holds personal spiritual and mass humanist (people in general) meanings.

- Description: two tall parallel vertical lines with two short branches making an X, connecting the top half of the vertical lines; resembles two Latin Ps in mirror image.

- Letter equivalent/sound: M

- Tree: holly

- Herb: madder

- Gemstone: garnet

- Color associations: red, silver

- Position in Futhark: 20

- Position in aett: 3:4

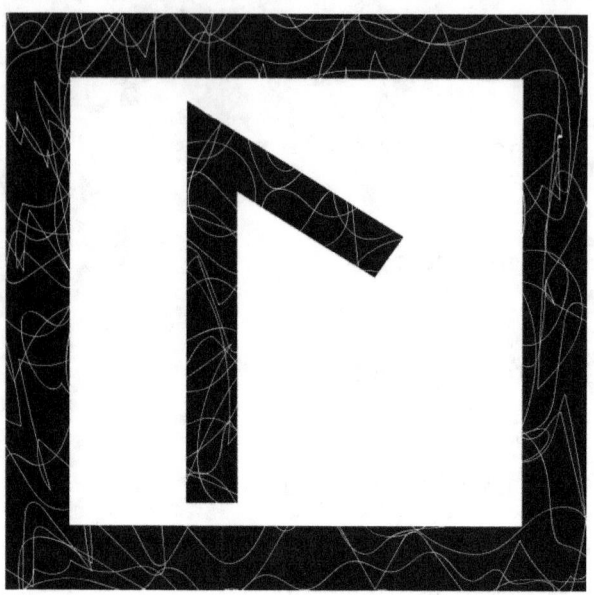

Lagu

- Meaning: lake; water

- This rune represents water as a source of deeper meaning and intuition. It represents the subconscious, imagination, dreams, and taps into psychic powers. It represents vital life energy as the source of life and is a symbol of fertility.

- Description: tall vertical line with a short branch aligned to the top of the vertical angling down to the right; resembles a lower-case Latin R(r).

- Letter equivalent/sound: L

- God: Njord

- Tree: willow

- Herb: leek

- Gemstone: pearl

- Color associations: green, black

- Position in Futhark: 21

- Position in aett: 3:5

Ing

- Meaning: Ing; fertility

- The god, Frey, was known to the Danes as the hero Ing. Ing was known for his sexual prowess. This rune represents male sexual energy as well as stored energy. It is connected with the creative spark, energy, and gestation.

- Description: four short branches make junctures at each end forming a parallelogram, a diamond shape; a variation of this rune appears as two Xs stacked has been adapted from the Anglo-Saxon Futhark; resembles a pointy Latin O.

- Letter equivalent/sound: Ng

- God: Ing/Frey

- Tree: apple

- Herb: gentian

- Gemstone: amber

- Color associations: yellow, brown

- Position in Futhark: 22

- Position in aett: 3:6

Daeg

- Meaning: day; hope, enlightenment

- Daeg represents the security found in light as opposed to the uncertainty of the dark. It is connected to consciousness and enlightenment, and mystical awakening as well as the more mundane concept that dawn will come again.

- Description: two tall parallel vertical lines with two long branches making an X, connecting the top of the left vertical line to the bottom of the right vertical line, and the bottom of the left vertical to the top of the right vertical; resembles two Latin Ds in mirror image.

- Letter equivalent/sound: D

- Tree: spruce

- Herb: clary sage

- Gemstone: diamond

- Color associations: blue, yellow

- Position in Futhark: 23

- Position in aett: 3:7

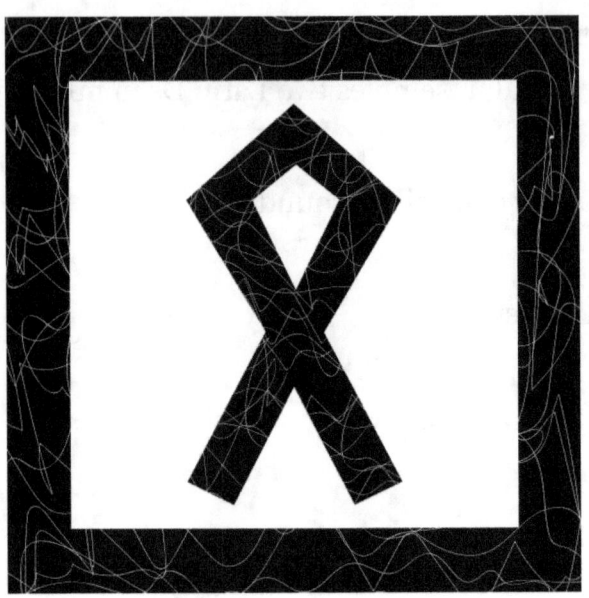

Odhal

- Meaning: home; inherited property

- This rune represents ancestral power and legacy. It holds connections with the home and domesticity. It is the embodiment of "home is where the heart is."

- Description: four short branches form a parallelogram, diamond shape, two short branches form "legs" angling down and away to the left and the right from the lowest point of the diamond shape; resembles a Latin X with a peaked roof.

- Letter equivalent/sound: O

- Tree: hawthorn

- Herb: clover

- Gemstone: ruby

- Color associations: dark yellow, brown

- Position in Futhark: 24

- Position in aett: 3:8

Runes take on additional meaning when they appear upside down, or when coming before or after another rune. In the next chapters, we will explore these additional meanings of runes when used in casting and divination.

Chapter Six: Rune Magic

Casting, or creating spells and amulets with runes is an attempt to tap into the magic of the Norns and have an impact on your fate. These are different practices from divination, where the runes provide answers to questions that can help you understand and learn of your fate.

Before you create a talisman or rune spells, take your time learning and becoming familiar with the runes. Memorize their names and meanings. Create pictures of the runes in your mind and breathe their names. When reading and writing runes, it is important to understand their meaning. Remember, runemasters needed to be well versed in the art and understanding of runes lest they unwittingly caused harm. Proceed with caution, especially if you are new to the pagan religions or a new practitioner of divination. There is a reason why runes continued into the modern era, and it wasn't due to its aspect of written language. Be aware of those energies.

Amulets

The simplest way to engage in rune magic is with an amulet. Amulets can be for your person or for larger areas, such as where you choose to practice your rune casting, an altar, a workspace, or your home. Personal amulets traditionally are a piece of jewelry featuring a guiding rune. This practice is not unlike Germanic warriors inscribing Tiwaz into their swords. They were not naming the sword for Tyr but were calling upon the energies of Tyr for strength and honor on the battlefield. Instilling the intention of the rune into a piece of jewelry will transfer those energies to you as you wear the amulet.

In your practice of gaining familiarity with the Elder Futhark, you may find that certain runes appear to you more often than others. Those runes' meanings resonate with you on a personal level that the other runes are not touching. Reflect on your understanding of those runes. They may need to be your first amulets.

You may find that different amulets need to be worn at different times. It may be that you need the energy of a specific rune more so during certain times. You may find wearing Ur will get you through a physical ordeal, such as running a marathon; or that Ing will calm you through a stressful waiting period; if you are a nervous traveler maybe you need Raidho.

Amulets can be a pendant worn around your neck, charms on a bracelet, and rings. Not everyone is comfortable wearing jewelry or displaying symbols in their jewelry. Amulets do not need to be worn but can be carried with you. Charms attached to a keyring, or carrying around a rune stone or stave in your pocket works as a way of keeping the amulet close.

Amulets don't have to be small. Wall hangings combining larger pieces featuring runes with regional fabrics, or painted tapestries work for larger spaces.

If you are arts and crafts oriented, you can make your own amulets. Follow the same instructions for creating a rune set with wood disks but drill a hole at the center top of the wood disk and add a jump ring so you can turn a rune stave into a pendant. To turn a glass rune stone into an amulet, glue the glass pebble into a bezel-set frame with a bail. Follow the same cleansing and preparatory steps discussed in the chapter on making your own runes if you choose to make your own. Remember to offer something to the powers of the runes in exchange for their wisdom.

Cleanse any rune jewelry or amulet you purchase. Cleanse it of the energies of the maker before you put it on display in your space. You want your rune to resonate with your energy, and not whatever was going on in the life of the artist when they created your new amulet. Same for if you purchase an amulet for someone. They may not be versed in the cleansing of energies, and unaware that they can be impacted by them. A good policy is to always cleanse magical energy gifts, and then touch the item as little as possible.

Bind runes

Bind runes are just what they sound like, the binding of runes: combining two or more runes for a power-packed talisman. Bind runes have been around since runestones first appeared. Most early examples of bind runes seemed to have been names, not unlike the Bluetooth logo. This logo is an example of a stacked bind rune using runes from the Younger Futhark to create a new symbol for the name Bluetooth— this was done intentionally as Bluetooth technology was named for Harald Bluetooth and was inspired by the ability to communicate at a distance that runestones provided during the Viking Age.

Stacked bind runes are a combination and layering of runes so they occupy the same space and create a new shape. By combining and redesigning the form this way, the energy and intention of the runes are joined, unlike in readings, where the order and position of any given rune influences the interpretations of other runes.

Layering Lagu over Isa creates a bind rune for good health. Ride and need combine as Raiho and Naudhiz come together forming a rune for safe travels. The joy of Wunjo and the gift of Gebo come together for a bound rune of love. There are many examples of bind runes already created. Many incorporate the runes in a way that is a little less straightforward than positioning one on top of another. Combining Ansur with Gebo creates a good luck symbol. The tall vertical of Ansur angles to the right and becomes one of the crossbars of the X of Gebo. A quick internet search will return many examples. With reflection on your needs and the meaning of runes, you can combine your own.

Same-stave bind runes build on the same central tall vertical line. The runes are stacked on top of each other, and where possible the lines overlap/combine into a new shape. An example of a same-stave rune appears on the Kylver Stone at the end of the Futhark. This rune is a combination of several Tiwaz and Ansur runes combined to form a protection rune.

Think of the properties you want to combine in your bind rune. If you need more than two runes, maybe the form will best be built from a same-stave bind rune or a radial bind rune.

Radial bind runes create a design where the vertical lines from a collection of runes extend to form a central junction; the runes radiate from a single point (not unlike the spokes of a wheel). This rune form has a similar appearance to Icelandic staves—centrally oriented sigils. Icelandic staves are not traditional rune forms, as they did not begin to appear in the historic record until well after the Viking Age. Even though not a traditional rune form, these radial runes have entered into contemporary practice. If your intuition guides you to radial forms, follow as the runes guide you.

As with all rune practice, when designing your bind runes, be present in your work. Focus on the intent of your bind rune when selecting which runes to incorporate. When creating runes to harness combined energies, your intuition and "gut feelings" must be listened to. If the energies from a bind rune don't feel right, something is trying to warn you that the combination isn't working. Destroy the rune you created, reflect on the outcome you desire, and try again.

Spellcasting

Unlike the protective or energy calling of a bind rune, rune scripts are messages to the Norns and guiding energies of our lives' directions. Writing fixes a concept into being. It exists now on a surface (be it paper or stone). While writing something down does not make it real, it definitely serves as an intention for that idea to be real within the universe.

Runes were a tool of fate, as the Norns used runes to direct the lives of those in the Nine Realms, as well as directing the health and wellness of Yggdrasil. Combining the intentions of writing and the directive forces of fate that are inherent in runes creates a script that announces to the powers of fate and the energies of the universe for a desired change or outcome.

Akin to casting your intentions forth, scripting runes creates more than simply wishes. They become directives for the ebb and flow of energies that surround you. Your life path, your fate, is not a constant linear line moving in a singular direction, there are twists and turns. With rune casting, you can let the controlling forces know which twists and turns you would like to proceed along.

These scripts should always be cast with positive intentions, lest fate is cruel and folds back on you with negative intent. These scripts should be temporary, and literally not carved in stone. Since these are written messages, it is important to understand the meaning of the runes you are using, and how they impact each other when used together.

Notice how the theme of knowing the runes, and understanding their meaning keeps reappearing when it comes to using them? Please spend time researching, reading, and meditating on the intentions and meanings of runes before engaging their energies for divination and magic.

Small spell scripts are made of a collection of runes, not unlike how one would read meanings into divination. What is not happening is a recipe or prose composed using runes as the letterforms. You are not spelling out words using runes as a replacement alphabet. You are combining concepts and meanings, not unlike a bind rune. Only, instead of combining shapes for a new design, you are spelling it out (literally and figuratively).

Transient natural materials work best for scripts. They combine the properties of being in the here now, yet are also not permanent, much like the energies you are attracting. As with rune staves/stones, the closer to nature and the World Tree your materials are, the more potent their energies: leaves, bark, paper.

After reflecting on the purpose of your rune script, determine what collection of runes will be best for your purpose. Gather your materials and compose your script. Paint or write your script. There are no set formulas, as each spell is specific and personal.

Keep your script with you for a few days. You may feel the need to charge your script in a full cycle of the sun before carrying it with you. After a few days, release the script back to the universe by burning it. Breathe the names of the runes and let them go.

Scripts can be composed for many purposes such as attracting success for a job interview, or love. There are no universal success or love spells. The energies you possess and the energies you seek differ from person to person, and expectation to expectation.

For example, to attract a feminine love (be that of a woman, or the nurturing aspect of feminine energy) you might consider Wunjo for happiness, Gebo for the gift of another, Eoh for partnership, and Feoh to increase the potency of the previous runes while also bringing in feminine energy. For a similar spell but calling for masculine energy or a man: Wunjo, Gebo, Ur, Eoh. By placing Eoh after Ur it binds the raw masculine energy into the partnership.

Chapter Seven: Divination and Reading Runes

Divination is the search for meaning from mystical sources. Reading runes is an attempt to gain that knowledge from the same sources that fed the World Tree and the Well of Wyrd - the source of the original runes. To seek knowledge from the runes is to ask from the source of the universe. Divination with runes is more about enlightenment and guidance than telling the future.

Understanding the runes

When using runes for magic and energy work you do not read them linearly. While they can serve as a form of alphabet, each shape representing a sound or part of language, that is not the case for this purpose.

Not only do you need to understand the foundation meaning of the individual runes, but you must also understand their placement in relation to each other.

When pulling runes for a reading or tossing them, the position, in the end, must be taken into the overall interpretation. Rune sets should be made one-sided so that only one direction for the symbol is ever created. A face-down rune has the exact meaning of a face-up rune. Simply flip the rune to be face up. When flipping, lift the piece left-to-right (or right-to-left), do not flip top-to-bottom (or bottom-to-top). That will reverse, or cause a merkstave, and will completely change the meaning of the reading.

When a rune appears in an upside-down orientation, that is called a merkstave and indicates a reversal or counter definition of the initial meaning. Merkstave does not necessarily carry a negative connotation. For the rune Thorn, merkstave can indicate a breaking down of barriers, which can be a positive interpretation. Eight of the runes have no merkstave position.

If a rune appears on its side, front facing up (for example, Beorc with the back of the shape lying flat and the two points in an upward position), simply rotate it into its normal right reading position. However, if the orientation of the rune symbol appears on its side and the symbol is front facing down (example Beorc with the back of the shape lying flat and the two points in a downward position), rotate the rune into its merkstave orientation. You are more likely to encounter this when tossing runes, or if your rune set is made up of symmetrical shapes without an obvious vertical orientation.

Interpretations

Feoh's interpretation of wealth can indicate the abundance of the previous rune/s in a layout. In the merkstave position, it can be interpreted as a loss.

Ur brings in virility, and its order of placement can add strength to the previous rune. In merkstave it can be interpreted as misguided stubbornness or negative health.

Thorn indicates defense, and it brings strength in understanding to previous runes. In merkstave it can indicate a breaking down of barriers or a betrayal.

Ansur is communication. In a position following other runes, it brings about a clarity of understanding of the previous runes. In merkstave it indicates miscommunications and manipulation.

Raidho represents the journey. Following other runes, it can mean a bringing in of those energies. In merkstave it indicates a disruption.

Kenaz is knowledge. When placed after other runes it can indicate a need to reinterpret those runes from a different perspective, so look with a creative eye. In merkstave it indicates a lack of forward thought, or a loss of intuition.

Gebo is a gift. Following other runes, it can indicate an abundance of those energies. It does not have a merkstave position.

Wunjo is joy, it brings a happy positive interpretation when placed after other runes. In merkstave, it is sadness.

Hagalaz represents a disruption. It is a change force no matter what its positioning is.

Naudhiz represents needs. When placed after other runes it can indicate a need to reflect on how the energies and attributes of the previous runes are desirable. It has no merkstave position.

Isa indicates stillness, a pause. When placed next to other runes it holds them in place. Isa has no merkstave position.

Gera is all about timing. Its influence on previous runes is about timing and sequence, indicating attention to the order of action. Gera does not have a merkstave position.

Eoh is the connection to spirituality. When placed after other runes it can indicate a reappearance of those energies. While technically it does not have a merkstave position, it can hold negative destructive meanings.

Peorth is the rune of luck. Its appearance after other runes can indicate taking a chance on what they present. In merkstave, it can indicate the negative aspects of gambling, addiction, lack of planning, and delusion.

Eolh is a strong protection rune. When placed next to other runes it can increase the potency of their energies. In merkstave, it can represent a loss of spiritual connectivity, hidden danger, and vulnerability.

Sowilo is a rune for joy and good health. It does not have a merkstave position.

Tiwaz brings honor. It adds strength to the runes it is placed after. In merkstave, it can represent analysis-paralysis and failure of action.

Beorc is a rune of birth. It brings a strong feminine energy of nurturing to the runes it is placed next to. In merkstave, it can represent loss, as well as relationship and fertility issues.

Ehwaz is partnership and trust. It combines the runes it appears next to, so that their energies work in tandem. In merkstave, it indicates mistrust and betrayal.

Mannaz is the rune of humankind. When in a position after other runes, its influence is about cooperation between and with the other runes. When in the merkstave position, it represents a negative bias against others, arrogance, and disappointment.

Lagu is tied to water and the ebb and flow of natural currents. When positioned following another rune, it provides a guiding influence. When it appears in the merkstave orientation, it indicates manipulation and poor judgment.

Ing can be sudden, forceful energy - it's a "bang." In conjunction with other runes, it can indicate a dramatic appearance and creative use of that rune's energy. There is no merkstave position for this rune.

Daeg brings hope. When used in conjunction with other runes it incorporates an element of certainty to their meanings. There is no merkstave orientation.

Odhal is the rune of heritage. It can bring a meaning of permanence when placed with other runes. In merkstave, it represents the loss of freedoms.

Remember when reading runes that their aett position also leads to their interpretation. Freya's aett indicates life cycle concepts, beginnings, coming together, and endings. The aett of Hagal is about external forces, the things beyond our control, while the runes in Tyr's aett are about the forces within, the things we have personal control over.

Reading the runes

Your intuition and your understanding of the runes will guide you to the most correct interpretation for that moment. When conducting a reading, you may want to spread a dedicated cloth for readings in front of you. Don't ask yes/no questions. Runes are not a magic eight-ball, and they will not give definite answers. They will not tell you to paint a room red instead of yellow, but they might provide encouragement for going to school to study law or medicine, for example. Request guidance for situations, concerns, and issues you may be experiencing.

Probably the easiest rune reading to do is a single stone pull. Simple questions work well with a single stone reading. Hold the bag of runes loosely in your grasp. Focus the intentions and energies of your concern into the runes. After a few steadying breaths, reach in and draw a single rune. Place the rune in front of you. Focus on this rune and what it means. How does it relate to your query? What are the aett forces behind the rune? Narrow in your focus and pay attention to your intuition.

If you are reading for someone else, have them hold the bag. They will place the rune in front of themselves. The orientation of the rune to them is the way to read it. (If you are sitting across from them, the rune will appear in the merkstave orientation to you. Remember to read it the way it appears to them.) You will need to know their question in order to properly understand the interpretation of the rune that comes to you. Asking for you to do a blind reading without understanding the nature of their query is game-playing, and the best you can do is give them a definition of the rune. It would be up to them to interpret its meaning for them. But for real guidance from the rune, you need to be able to interpret the greater meanings each rune holds. The other person doesn't have to share what they are requesting from the runes until after their selection has been revealed.

Layouts for readings

Layouts that follow the forms of the rune shape will pull on the overwhelming energy of that rune. Laying runes in an overall Tiwaz shape will pull on the energy of honor and doing the right thing in conflict with Tyr. Thus, your reading may be cast in a direction of self-sacrifice for the greater good of the situation that the reading is regarding. Peorth can be seen as the rune of fate, but since it is also the rune of mystery and gambling, it can bring an aspect of chaos into your reading.

Layouts with the number three as a base tap into the energy of the runes the strongest. The Well of Wyrd was the divine source of knowledge that Odin stared into for nine days. There are three Norns. There are Nine Realms.

Runes for these readings can be tossed into a small pile and selected at random while looking up or away from the runes. Or they can be pulled directly from their bag.

There are two distinct three-rune readings. As their name indicates, they involve three runes. The first layout creates a top-down column. The top/first position of the first rune represents the *here* and *now*. The second rune is placed below the first. The position of the second rune represents the *path* you are on. The position of the third rune at the base of the column represents the *goal/future*.

The second three-rune layout is right to left. The first rune position represents an *overview* of the situation. The second rune, placed to the left, represents a *challenge* or *problem*. The third rune is placed to the left of the second (now middle) rune. This rune represents the *course of action*, and how that rune interacts with the previous runes provides insight into the overall message of the other runes.

A simple six-rune reading takes the layout of the first three-rune layout mentioned above, but the runes are read in pairs. The first two runes are placed next to each other in the top *here/now* position. The second pair is placed in the *path* position. And the last two in the bottom *goal/future* position. The combination of the pairs provides an additional layer of information to interpret.

Another variation of this layout is a nine-rune spread. Pick three runes at a time, for the three positions of *here/now, path,* and *goal/future.* In the groupings of three, each rune impacts the others in its grouping. This variation provides for a more in-depth interpretation of the guiding energies from the runes.

Sometimes referred to as an Odin's cross, this simple cross reading uses five runes. It starts with a single rune that will become the center point of the cross spread. This first rune represents the *present.* The second rune is placed to the left, in the *past* position. The third rune is placed to the right of the *present* rune, into the *future* position. The fourth rune to be placed goes below the *center/present* rune. In this position, it signifies a *hindrance* to what is being queried. The final rune is placed above the *center/present* rune in the *help* position.

The Thor's Hammer spread is a nine-rune layout. The nine positions of this spread reveal personal truths. The first rune is placed at the base of the configuration, and it represents the face you show the world. The second rune is placed a row above and to the left. This one reveals your inner fears. Rune three, placed on the second row and to the right of center is what you are looking for. The fourth rune is placed another row higher than runes two and three, but is directly aligned with the first rune. It will provide the guidance for approaching this reading. The fifth rune is placed directly above the fourth rune. It provides insight into what you hope to become. Rune positions five through nine create a cross pattern, with positions seven and nine lining up with runes one, four and five.

The sixth rune, a row above and to the left of center, addresses what forces are hindering your progress. Rune seven is placed in the center position of the same row, and it is your destiny. Rune eight is positioned to the right of the seventh rune and regards what you need to learn in order to find your true self. The ninth and final rune is placed top and center. It is your true self. As you can see from the meanings of the nine positions, this spread digs deep into self and psyche.

Layouts can also follow the ones used for traditional Tarot card readings. Your interpretations of the runes for different spreads will be more complex depending on the complexity of the layout.

Tossing of the runes leaves the reading open to much more personal interpretation. Unlike a guided layout, where each position holds a meaning, the free form landing of runes is open to what your intuition is telling you. Your interpretation may guide you that runes that land face down do not wish to be included in the reading.

Pay attention to runes landing in the merkstave position, and which ones are not quite merkstave or not quite upright. Notice which runes are touching, or clustered together. There is no direction order that the runes must be read, so you will have to determine that for yourself.

When conducting readings for others, the runes need to tune into their energies. Be sure to cleanse your runes regularly between reading if possible. You don't want one person to leave an overwhelming energy residue that could influence all readings after. The dominating energy of your rune set should be from you. As you grow more comfortable in using runes and handling your personal rune sets, you'll be able to sense when your runes have a taint or residue from another energy source.

Final Words

Thank you for making it to the end of this book. I hope you have enjoyed learning the basics about runes, their long history, and how they can be used for a variety of purposes.

If you would like to learn more and dive deeper into the world of runes and Norse mythology, translations of the *Poetic Edda* and the old rune poems are available online from several sources. Keep in mind that the versions available online are translations of translations, and that the original writings were most likely done by monks. So, while the original poem– the pre-Christian, oral tradition version– would not have the Christian references, the translations might.

When learning about and working with any religious/magic tradition, please remember to do so in a respectful manner. Runes belong to the Old-World Gods, whose practices and traditions have changed over the centuries, so be mindful of what we do know about their original intentions and context. As you continue to learn more about runes, you will gain your own wisdom regarding their meanings.

Image Credit: Shutterstock.com

www.ingramcontent.com/pod-product-compliance
Lightning Source LLC
Chambersburg PA
CBHW071019120626
46546CB00003B/1162